LIVING LIFE MEDITATIVE WAY

Achieving Big Sooner or Later-Magically (Part 1 of 2)

KHAGESH MAHANTA

PREFACE

"Remaining Meditative at every situation and occasion is a great art we need to master at."

Imagine a situation when there is a good flow of happiness to your heart when you are in a peaceful valley with limitless greenery, colorful blossomed flowers, fragrances, the utmost serenity, superb curvilinear shapes of the horizon all around, and a gentle breeze that can soothe you.

But what about your happiness when you come back to harsh reality and your mind travels through a state of turbulence due to numerous distractions from all around? The fact is that going to the cave of a mountain and escaping the realities of family, society, and professional life may not be a good solution for most of us.

Obviously, distractions tend to interrupt and obstruct our work or advancements badly, making us frustrated and stressed. Then what is the way through which we can not only win over the distractions and also go ahead to achieve big things and remain genuinely happy? One of the correct answers will be "Meditative way".

"Will it be difficult to follow the path?" Another question may arise.

The correct and direct answer will be: "Not at all." In fact, that is a natural way. In most cases, we need to go back to the original state of the self.

The biggest advantage everyone has is that their original nature is to remain calm and stable. As the distractions will be present all the time, more or less, irrespective of whether you like them or not, the winning strategy will be to get trained to be in the original state, known as "The meditative state."

In this book, we will explore how to remain meditative in diverse situations, remain happy, and achieve big things.

A NOTE

Through practice, if you can master the art of remaining at the meditative state all the time, you will be able to maintain a constant flow of happiness in your mind in all situations. Your mind will be at peace all the time, and you will be able to focus on whatever you do or get engaged in.

In such a state of mind, you can achieve big things and remain happy, relaxed, stable, and cool.

A CONFESSION

I initially wrote the book for myself so that by reading my own experiences and feelings that I gathered through observations in different personal, professional, and social situations and occasions, I could enhance my level of focus, maintain coolness and happiness, and facilitate enhancing my ability to work during various distractions.

Later on, I felt that both books of the series would be helpful for all.

DEDICATED TO

My beloved mother ("Maa") Mrs. Manomati Mahanta, for her unconditional love, care, and continuous encouragement.

COPYRIGHT AND DISCLAIMER

Copyright © 2021 by Khagesh Mahanta.

Author: Khagesh Mahanta.

Self-published by: Khagesh Mahanta.

Year of First Publishing: 2021.

Cover Design: By Khagesh Mahanta.

Book Type: Paperback.

Revision Level: 02

This book is the result of the author's observations, experiments, and experiences and is his original work. Any resemblance to anyone else's event or work is unintentional. The purpose of this book is to help people overcome stresses, win distractions, and facilitate a constant flow of happiness in millions of hearts.

Every sentence written in the book is written with an honest purpose and with no intention to hurt anybody's feelings, faiths, or notions.

The methods included in the book may not be the definite solutions to somebody's problems or pains, even though the motive is to help all.

Readers are requested to apply their own judgments before trying any method included in the book, even though it is expected that the methods will be beneficial to them.

No method described in the book can be a substitute for the standard medical treatment for disease, including stress-related complications.

REMAINING MEDITATIVE WHILE FACING USUAL OR OFFBEAT CHALLENGES

Chapter 1: When someone misunderstands you and you are not able to make that person understand.

It's normal to have a misunderstanding in the mind of some other person about you. You attempted but were unsuccessful in making her/ him understand.

Run this thought through your mind: You will be able to remove the cloud of misunderstanding from the person's mind.

Never argue or wrestle with the individual. Sit down calmly and take note of the subject of the misunderstanding as well as the possible causes. Focus on each possible cause and write down the possible solutions that have come to your mind. Choose some people around you and consider their perspectives in similar situations.

When you are clear about the problem and your mind is in a stable and cool state, you are able to focus on finding the best possible solution options.

In that state of mind, propose the person for a face-to-face or online discussion. Whenever the person agrees to have a discussion with you, first listen to her or him with full concentration and patience. She or he may react in a rough way, but, being in the meditative state, you will maintain the same cool state.

After completely listening to her/his points, including complaints and grievances, it is your turn to offer your solutions in a very cool, simple, and decent way.

There is a solution to every problem or issue. Run with positive thoughts to resolve the issue.

The person may directly accept one of your proposals or may give a revised proposal based on your proposal. If your mind is open and you are ready to adjust without hampering your self-esteem, then the person may get clarity about her or his doubt.

Continue your efforts with huge patience so that a solution may come your way. If you feel the need, you may take the help of someone whom you feel is in a better meditative state.

When misunderstanding goes away, sit down cool and analyze what lesson you have learned from the issue and note down the possible ways on how to prevent such situation in the future.

In fact, every time someone misunderstands you and you are not able to make her/him understand, instead of getting frustrated and irritated, run the positive strong thought in your mind that you will either discover or invent a better way of looking at yourself to diagnose the causes of the misunderstanding.

****

Chapter 2: When people around you insult you for daring to start something that others consider impossible.

The golden rule will be to accept the insults in a positive way.

You may have visualized and assessed the difficulty in achieving your dreams and may have already set your goals accordingly, started walking, or gone ahead to reach the destination. You may have already made yourself mentally prepared to face any challenge and developed your strategy. And also, you may have made yourself ready to walk on fire to reach your cherished goals.

However, for others who are either in their own comfort zones or in different states of mind, it may be normal to regard your dreams as crazy. They may not imagine how strong and determined you are or how amazing your dreams may be!

When people around you are not able to perceive the seriousness of your crazy thoughts and activities, they may usually make fun of them.

It is futile to educate others on how good and achievable your dreams and goals are. Simply focus on the goals you have set for yourself in accordance with your dreams and you will be unstoppable, regardless of whether others around you praise or laugh at you.

Through regular practice, when you are able to keep your mind in the meditative state, irrespective of whether others ridicule or praise you, there will be a flow of happiness and joy in your mind, as your focus will be on achieving big things and your mind will be able to foresee the fulfillment of your aspirations.

All will surely follow and give you a hero's welcome after you turn your dreams into reality in a grand way.

****

Chapter 3: When you are performing a task where others have high expectations of you and a minor distraction can wreak havoc.

There should be a continuous flow of happiness in your mind because so many people have so much trust and hope in you!

Instead of worrying about "What will happen," focus on and act on your task.

Practice will truly make perfect, and you will never have to struggle to decide where to hit the ball in order for it to cross the goalposts and touch the net.

You cannot afford to be distracted, even for a moment, as even a distraction of one millisecond may cause havoc. The high expectations of others for you should motivate you to remain focused and bring a constant stream of happiness to your mind.

Can you take a chance to get distracted for a moment? The big answer is "Never."

Can the rotation of the earth around the sun be stopped or distracted for a millisecond? The true answer is "No."

Can your heart stop beating for a moment? The big and only true answer is "No."

And is there anybody to motivate the earth to rotate around the sun or the heart to beat continuously? The answer will be "No."

The most powerful motivating factor you have is that there are so many expectations and goodwill for you to keep you going all the time! The expectation and goodwill of others will make your dreams brighter and your confidence level higher.

****

Chapter 4: When you fail in your mission again and again.

If you fail in your mission again and again, none of those failures will be called a failure unless you accept that you have failed.

Actually, you did not fail, but we're trying to find and walk on the path that could lead you to your destination. This thought will prompt you to try again and again. Finally, you will walk on the path that will directly lead you to your destination, and that experience of success will help you achieve other missions in easier and better ways.

Every time you fail in the mission, sit down in a calm manner and make a list of the lessons that you have learned from your last attempt. Do this as many times as you fail. Every new lesson that is learned must be added to the list. The lessons will be analyzed, and corrective as well as preventive actions will be taken against every reason for failure based on the learning.

Find a web in a garden, a park, or anywhere that was started by a spider. Pay close attention and observe what the spider is doing.

See how the spider accepts so many failures with positivity and tries again and again until it finally makes its web, the design of which is so beautiful and well interwoven! In nature, you will find so many brilliant examples of building castles out of so many failures.

When you are deeply in love and can feel that love all the time for your desired goals, the intermediate setbacks are unimportant.

****

Chapter 5: When you are in legal trouble, even though you are innocent.

It's extremely important to keep your mind stable and cool whenever you are in a critical situation.

"I am innocent, and so I will surely overcome the situation." If you are confident and honest about your innocence, you must run this positive thought through your mind completely. You are facing legal difficulty because of some wrong perceptions or foul motives on the part of some individuals or organizations.

You are just victimized by someone else's wrong perceptions or foul motives. It's possible to bring out the truth by applying the correct strategy while maintaining coolness and calm and remaining confident of proving your righteousness with competent legal authority.

While accumulating evidence for furnishing with authority, you will be relieved with the happy thought that, irrespective of all the false blemishes, you can stand as clean and powerful. Such situations in life teach everyone, for the good, the lesson of remaining alert all the time. A small loophole exposed to others may cause a mess.

The power of innocence is tremendous. You will never allow any false allegation to overpower your innocence, as that will set a wrong trend against the universal truth that "Truth always triumphs" in the long run.

Let the mind accept the bitter truth that even after being cautious and keeping yourself away from illegal things, a situation may arise accidentally without your knowledge. A mental state of stability, focus, and coolness helps you better ease out of such accidental falls.

****

Chapter 6: When you have a valid point but nobody around you agrees to it.

Keep calm with the following thoughts:

- You have an opportunity to re-check your point that you would not have had if we had all agreed to it.
- You still have the opportunity to improve the way you represent or express your point in a group, so that next time it may be easier for others to understand how good and useful your point is.
- The points of view of others may, in fact, be better than yours.
- You are intelligent and have a new positive challenge to explore better ideas.

The aforesaid thoughts will keep you from getting irritated or making the situation worse.

Regardless of the preceding thought, if you continue to receive negative comments from others as a result of your point, remain positive and composed, and do your mental preparation with patience and perseverance to better lead yourself.

When you are open to remaining positive and composed, things will improve.

****

REMAINING MEDITATIVE WHILE HANDLING AWKWARD SITUATIONS

Chapter 7: When you are left with nothing.

Apparently, you may be left with nothing. You may be without a job or maybe bankrupt; your business may have been crushed down, or you may have lost your beloved ones. But, while digging inside, you will discover that you are still a powerhouse of so many intangible assets, by dint of which you can shine again like a diamond!

The state of being "Left with nothing" is actually an opportunity to build an empire of innumerable things.

When you are apparently left with nothing, you actually come out of your comfort zone. Coming out of your comfort zone is a sign that you have accepted the challenge of life. There will be numerous aches and pains as a result of losing everything through no fault of your own.

A big challenge is in front of you: "To achieve many things out of nothing."

Run this positive thought again and again in your mind, knowing that you can overcome whatever the level of difficulty may be. Read the sentences that motivate you; display the motivational posters that help to keep you strong. Listen to the motivational sentences of the best motivational speakers.

You do not have time to get de-motivated. List all the things that you can do. From that list, you will understand how skilled you are. Now, filter out all the activities that you love to do. As you are going to achieve many things out of nothing, you will have to choose a few things that you love the most and that can solve any problem areas. If you love work, you can write about your high dreams again. Whenever there will be lots of perspiration to achieve your new aspirations, you will be able to maintain a continuous flow of happiness and peace in your mind. You will keep on discovering more and more of the beautiful "inner you."

When you start striving again, you will understand that more and more avenues are being opened and widened. After you achieve a good height, you will find that all your friends and relatives who went away when you were "Left with nothing" will come back to you and will express how much they love you. Forgive everyone for coming nearer to you again after maintaining big distances during your bad days. Send your best wishes to all of them.

When you put your regular and sincere efforts into remaining in the meditative state, the apparent physical state of "I am left with nothing" will not be able to adversely affect you, as your mind will remain full of so many positive thoughts and enhanced vision (to clearly see the potentials and possibilities ahead of you) that you will surely take up the big challenges instead of remaining in a vague state of confusion!

****

Chapter 8: When you discover that you entered into a relationship with a wrong person.

Even after being careful and alert, sometimes you may enter into a relationship with a person whose approaches are unethical or whose wavelengths or chemistry don't match yours.

Remain cool and light. All the time, keep in mind that unless something is clearly defined by the law as "Illegal" or "Illogical", in all other cases, the right or wrong of something depends on your perspective. So, in a gentle way, verify whether her or his approach is really unethical or apparently so. Keep in mind that nobody in the world is perfect. Keep positive thoughts about the person at all times and try to persuade her or him that an ethical approach to doing the same or similar thing that she or he is doing is preferable.

To match the wavelength of the person, adopt the policy of adjustment, as long as the principle of your life is not jeopardized. Sit down and assess where you stand in terms of ethics and adaptability. Discuss with her/him as many times as you feel comfortable, bringing out necessary changes for better compatibility. Your cool and calm approach may help to bring a better result. Even if she or he reacts rudely and negatively to your conversations and approaches, keep your cool and avoid any tussles with the person.

You are making sincere and full-hearted efforts to get the situation better. You will have full faith that changes for the better are always possible and that the differences can be sorted out amicably.

Through your goodwill and wishes, the person who is judged as "Wrong" may appear to shift towards "Right."

Keep wishing her or him well, silently and wholeheartedly.

If, after adopting the positive approach, she or he still remains the "Wrong" person in your view, then it's better to depart or to keep distance with the mutually agreed arrangement.

You can still continue to wish her or him the best.

****

Chapter 9: While driving on a dangerous road.

You may not like to take your vehicle on a road where there is the danger of an accident or an undesirable event at every step. So, at any cost, you would like to avoid the road. But there may be a situation where you need to use the road.

"I am going to cross the road safely." You will run the positive, firm thought through your mind continuously, again and again. All your preparation will be based on that thought.

You and your co-passengers will remain alert and maintain silence. Your focus will be on the road, on every meter of the distance you are going to cross, and on the planned exit path.

When the road is full of bumps and potholes:

Mentally, be ready to move very slowly and enjoy the ups and downs caused by the unevenness of the road. Find the rhythms in the jumps and the jerks. While enjoying the ride, check your rearview mirrors for other cars in your rear and on the sides so you can give way to the over taker. At the same time, observe the front road, especially the bumps and the potholes in front of you, and choose better ones.

When the road is on a hill and is zigzagged with big hanging rocks on one side and a steep slope on the other side:

You need to take your car forward, with a constant vigil on all four sides around your vehicle. There may be landslides; big hanging rocks may come down with the land; there may be an obstruction on the road, partially blocking the road. It's required to keep a sufficient margin on the other side of a steep slope, where a slight mistake may take your vehicle straight down thousands of feet. Keep constant vigil, with the single positive challenge of crossing the road safely.

When it's too dark all around and the whole road is fully deserted:

As you cannot avoid the road nor stay stagnant, the only option left is to go ahead with focused, constant vigilance. Your car lights will be on, and whenever required, you and the co-travelers will be in the "Ever-ready" status to keep the torches on and make calls to the emergency helpline numbers. You are able to see the front obstructions, if any, and are able to see if some human beings or animals are approaching your vehicle. All the windows of your vehicle will remain fully closed. You will drive slowly to keep control of every undesirable emergency.

You'll keep running with the positive thought in your head that you're safe and will stay safe the whole way.

Your focus will still be on your desired exit pathway.

****

Chapter 10: When you are fired from your job.

Feel relieved that you've been fired. You are definitely going to seize a better opportunity. And because of the fact that you are fired, you have become open to so many better avenues. So, convey your appreciation to all who were directly or indirectly involved in your firing.

Allow your thoughts to become so large in your mind that you gain the ability to take on a new and massive challenge that no intermittent discomfort can disturb or deviate you. The world is so big! There are so many options! So, there is no point in losing heart after getting fired.

Remaining cool and composed is of utmost importance.

If you were performing your work efficiently but became the victim of someone's dirty politics or misunderstanding, clearly express your points to the concerned authority with full honesty. However, be kind to those who used dirty politics against you or misunderstood you.

If you made a serious or multiple mistakes while carrying out the assignments, or if you failed to complete the tasks because you lacked the necessary knowledge, skill, and experience, accept full responsibility for your actions and pledge to improve yourself as soon as possible.

Consider the experience of being fired from a job as a beautiful lesson learned. Many times, you even get excited about an ongoing job when you understand that the job is neither interesting nor useful nor your cup of tea.

The truth is that the same person can reach the pinnacle of success in one job but sink in another.

Sit down in silence at a suitable place and at a suitable time when you can be in deep thought about exploring your unutilized or partly utilized inner potentials.

Do that exercise at regular intervals. You will be amazed to discover the "Inner You."

When you will start utilizing your hidden potentials, the incidence of getting sacked from jobs will become too minute and your need for jobs at others' favors will vanish forever.

****

Chapter 11: When another person becomes ready to fight with you.

Someone is ready to fight with you because some of your actions or behaviors in the present or past have made her or him annoyed.

You may be at fault, or your actions or behaviors may be wrongly interpreted or perceived.

But, whatever the facts, your immediate action will be to change the environment of a fight to a calm and quiet one.

Whatever the situation may be, you will have to remain cool and composed. Run a positive thought about the person.

If you are at fault, admitting the fault with a big "Sorry," giving a commitment to not repeating such incidents, and if required, offering compensation for the wrong act that you have committed, may help to alleviate the situation.

If you are innocent but the person has wrongly perceived you, you must clearly and straightaway tell her or him about the misunderstanding or wrong perception, in a soft yet firm and cool way.

Making jokes, silently ignoring her or him, or reacting with your hot temper may aggravate the situation. At the time when the person is annoyed and starts emanating the fire of anger, you need to act as an extinguisher.

When the fire of her/his annoyance is not given a favorable environment to grow, the situation will improve over time.

Another important thing is to protect you from getting hurt by other people's aggression when the situation becomes or remains hot.

If the person has become a fireball out of an extremely hot temper, it is always better to maintain a safer distance, take the help of someone else, or get away from the scene until the situation comes back to a controllable level.

In this case, getting away is a wise decision. You will still maintain your cool and wish well for that person without any adverse reaction. The person will soon develop a better feeling for you and will even start regretting that, even after so much aggression and misbehavior, you kept on doing good and maintained your cool. "Hot" definitely becomes "Cold" if you continue to remain cool and composed and act to make the situation better.

****

Chapter 12: When you see your decent friend in an awkward and unexpected situation.

You have seen him heavily drunk, with a bottle in his hand, walking on the road inconsistently. He was an occasional mild drinker, as per your knowledge, and was a perfect gentleman. Such a scene is surprising for you, but if you ignore the matter as if nothing has happened, the situation may worsen for your friend. And you have social and moral responsibilities for your friend.

You may hold on, sit, or stand for a moment. Deep breathe, and proceed to your friend with a good thought in your mind. Reach him, taking good care of your safety, and greet him with a warm smile, coming to the roadside. Take him to your house or a comfortable place and let him rest for some time. In that process, he may use foul language, being in an inebriated state. But you will remain calm and quiet and try to understand what led him to drink so heavily. Wait till he returns to normalcy from his drunken state, and then deliver your best possible motivational speech to help him out.

During that process, try to understand his pain points. Your cool and calm posture will help your friend improve his mental state. You may share some of your personal pains that you have healed or are going to heal. Also, if possible, share your experiences with how others have reduced similar pain.

Let there be full patience. After he feels a little better, it's better to take him to a nearby rehabilitation center.

Your cool and thoughtful disposition and patience will surely have a positive effect on the mind of your friend. Develop yourself so much that you can teach your friend how to meditate and how to remain genuinely happy and peaceful, even in difficult situations.

KHAGESH MAHANTA

****

Chapter 13: When your beloved child develops a serious mental health problem.

She or he might have come across many fights in her or his mind due to so many reasons, some of which may be the repeatedly running scenes in her or his mind of your past tussles with your spouse or some disturbing scenes or incidences either in reality or in the movies. She or he may be stressed and disturbed as a result of so many expectations placed on her or him by others, as well as follow-ups on matters pertaining to her or his studies, competitive exams, or future careers, or on matters that may be stressful or hateful to her or him.

Whatever her or his unexpected mental problem is, you must remain focused on the fact that she or he requires constant love and care from you and your spouse. You'll need a lot of patience to put up with her or his erratic and unpleasant behaviors and conversations.

Every morning, you will think of her or him and wish him or her the best of luck for the day. She or he should be aware of your love and concern throughout the day. Never allow a situation to arise that causes her or him to become more tense. Even if you foresee the onset of such a situation, take full control of yourself so that she or he does not get exposed to the stresses related to the situation.

Her or his recovery could take a long time, or the mental illness could last the rest of his or her life. But your positive approach will help you manage everything in a cool way. From time to time, she or he may start behaving and working normally, but you cannot be overly optimistic that she or he has recovered from her or his mental health problem. Allow her/his medication and counseling to continue on a regular basis, in accordance with the routine and review results by the relevant specialists.

The more positive and calm you remain, the faster and better her or his mental healing will be.

****

Chapter 14: When you are ill.

Your illness may be due to the fact that some microorganism is able to overpower your internal defense mechanism, or some mental stress may be able to start disturbing the equilibrium in your mind.

Run this positive thought inside you: you are going to win over your illness.

You may choose and continue with a parallel treatment option with the fewest side effects, but the most important thing is your inner confidence and determination to fight the illness.

Your full concentration will be on the intake of the immunity-boosting foods as well as continuing with the amazingly lovely thought, "No illness can remain stagnant inside me."

Relax after loosening your hands and feet and focusing on your deep breathing in and out at regular intervals while lying down in your bed.

Every day, whenever you can, look at the horizon, where the sky and the earth meet. If you cannot walk or move, move virtually deep inside to look at the horizon. In both cases, go so deep that the inner light of hope can wash away the gloomy or pessimistic thoughts from you.

At night, when it is dark outside, lie down under the clear, open sky and look at the magnificent scenes that are getting better continuously, as well as the limitless stars. Feel that the flow of happiness has come in and has washed down all the toxins from inside you.

At dawn and dusk, look at the outstanding sun as a lovely ball of inspiration.

When a lawn of grass is full of so many pearls of dew, just walk through it barefooted and absorb all the happiness.

When all of your happy hormones are balanced in your body, you will recover from your illness faster.

The strong feeling of happiness inside you will make your internal healing system more active and stronger.

****

Chapter 15: When someone you have helped cheats you instead of acknowledging your help.

It is extremely difficult, but possible, to keep your cool and forgive the person who has cheated you.

But, at the same time, it is very useful to understand what led the person to cheat you. For example, the person may be financially broke, and even though she or he wanted to return the money borrowed from you, she or he might not be able to do that.

Whatever the reason, send her or him all your best wishes in the hope that he or she realizes his or her wrongdoing.

The most important benefit of being cheated is the lesson learned, which will allow you to be more alert in the future. If you can keep your mind alert while focusing on your work and missions, no one else will be able to fool you because of the precautions you take.

Helping other people will still be in your heart and blood. However, because you are determined not to give others another chance to defraud you, you will construct a firewall around you that will work for you while you keep yourself busy delivering your work and serving others.

Have the positive thought in your mind that you are going to make up for the loss that happened because of the deceitful act of some other person.

Another important thought that you will have is that you will strive for more self-sufficiency. Accordingly, spread the message everywhere about being interdependent instead of simply dependent.

If someone deliberately cheats you despite your help, take on the challenge of empowering and enriching yourself in such a way that such acts by others cannot harm you in any way. At that stature of yours, you will always be ready to help others as much as possible—even more than before—but will be in a better position not to expect anything from anyone.

****

Chapter 16: When you know that you are going to die soon.

You and your near and dear ones know about the medical declaration made by one or more competent medical authorities that you are going to die soon. But keep this firm belief in your mind: the way you have kept yourself alive till now, with the same spirit, you will remain alive tomorrow also, despite all the probabilities of dying.

Can a prediction about your imminent death make you a "Dead person"? Never allow yourself to make that happen. Run with the positive thought that you are going to live and rise. Your body can be rejuvenated; each and every organ of your body can undergo rejuvenation. Accept your pains and begin playing happily with them. At this critical time, let others think and say what they want to. But you will never say the word "Die."

When you have heard of the prediction(s) made by the competent medical authority (or authorities) that you are going to die soon, you have all the right to make fresh attempts to stay alive. Conduct extensive research, and then choose the best-proven alternative natural treatments, whatever they may be. Let such searches, research, and treatments run in full swing.

Instead of stopping and looking down when your alternate treatments and new attempts at recovery continue, get involved with full dedication to the work you love. Run as much as you can towards achieving your cherished life aspirations.

Whenever happy hormones start getting extracted in your body in a balanced way to make you energetic, miracles may start happening. Never, ever say or allow the thought of death to enter your mind and demoralize you.

With your positive thoughts and stability of mind, the flow of happiness will continue to remain in your mind, even at such a critical stage of life. With that approach, you have the potential to greatly extend your alive state.

Even after all those, if you die, "Die happily," as death is a compulsory part of life and the ultimate truth.

****

Chapter 17: When you misplace your wallet, which contained all of your credit and debit cards as well as your ID.

Sit down and take deep breaths to remain cool. In that state of mind, close your eyes and try to remember where you kept your wallet after you last opened or saw it. While keeping your eyes closed and continuing your slow, deep breath, try to remember when you last took out some of the cards, IDs, or cash from your wallet.

When your mind is stable and cool, you are able to bring many past events or things to your memory. Sitting down in a comfortable manner or lying down with your face up and your hands relaxed is a better way to focus and may help you locate your wallet.

By continuing with the aforesaid practice, you may be able to mentally travel and virtually reach your wallet. The practice may run repeatedly for some time. And your success depends on the level of serenity in your mind. When your mind discovers a clue while travelling virtually, you can physically try to follow it or enlist the help of another trustworthy person to check onsite.

With mental focus, you can go to any depth and discover what is hidden. That is not only the case with your wallet but also with everything. Many things that were previously impossible to trace in a normal situation will come to the fore with clear features, such as those of crystals, one after the other if your mind can fully focus while remaining calm and quiet.

After some repeated efforts with focus, if your wallet is still untraceable, you may go ahead with other actions like blocking your cards and deactivating your IDs so that others cannot misuse them. You can still send your good thoughts to the person who may have stolen your wallet. Such continuous and deep thought may help to bring good thoughts into the mind of that person and convince them to return your wallet.

****

REMAINING MEDITATIVE WHILE SETTING PRIORITIES

41

Chapter 18: While focusing on a few things of higher importance.

There are so many activities in front of you, and time is short. If you think about it, there are only a few key activities that can help you achieve the majority of your life's goals.

With full focus and dedication, pick up only those few activities having the potential of making prime value addition.

You will make your plan that will be unique because you are unique in this world. Nobody can be identical with you in terms of your body parts, the horizon of your mind, your capability, interests, and ambitions.

In a fully focused mind, make a to-do list of all the tasks that you can accomplish. Let it take as much time as required to complete the list.

Add the new column, with the name "New1," to the list, with the drop-down list of "Yes" and "No," and with the following heading: "Is the task harmful for the society?"

Add another column, with the name New2, to the list, with the following heading:

"The goals that you want to reach at."

Make a drop-down list of all the goals.

Add the new column 3, with the name New3, and the following heading:

"How important is the task?"

Make the drop-down list range from 1 to 10.

Add the new column 4, with the name "New4", with the following heading: "How urgent the task is."

Make the drop-down list range from 1 to 10.

Add a new column, "New5", with the following heading: "How rewarding the task is."

Make the drop-down list range from 1 to 10.

If the value of Column "New1" is "yes" for a task, simply eliminate the task.

Or, if you are not able to put a value on a task in new column 2 ("New2"), then eliminate the task.

If all the values in the new columns New3, New4, and New5 are below 5, then put the task in quarantine.

After completing the aforesaid practices, you will see that the majority of the activities that were included in your To Do Task List are gone from the list, leaving only a few. Those few will be your key tasks, with the ability to produce prime results.

Your updated, active To-Do list is the concise one that you can focus on and sustain while working on your life's goals.

****

REMAINING MEDITATIVE WHILE STARTING THE DAY

44

Chapter 19: When you get up in the morning.

As soon as you wake up from your sleep, fill your heart with positivity. A really soothing morning meditation soundtrack at a low volume may help with that.

The following step-by-step activities will help to maintain a positive state of mind:

- Keep your body lying in a relaxed way, with your back touching the bed for at least one minute, your hands and feet completely free and loose, and your eyes closed.
- Rub both of your palms vigorously and keep both palms on both eyes.
- Repeat the above step at least five times to make your lovely eyes ready to open.
- While keeping the warm palms loosely on your eyes, open your eyes slowly.
- Slowly and steadily rotate your whole body to the left side while still lying down and keeping your hands and feet free.
- Bring yourself into a sitting position using your hands, slowly and steadily, without jerking, and without injuring your body.
- Relax for one minute in this sitting position.
- Take out both of your feet and let those touch the floor, slowly and steadily, and sit with your back straight.
- Slowly and steadily, deep breathe in and deep breathe out at least five times.
- Slowly drink a glass of warm water in that sitting position.
- Slowly stand up without any abrupt jerks. Say "Thank you" to the almighty from your heart for giving you the opportunity to stand up.
- Proceed to the bathroom to empty your bowels and bladder.

- Fill up your mouth with drinking water and splash clean water (first a little warm, then slightly cold) at least twenty times. Keep the thought of love in your eyes: "With the help of my eyes, I am able to see the beautiful world and the sky."
- Brush the teeth with a suitable brush and paste. While brushing, keep the thought in your mind that, because of the teeth, you are able to grind your food for your stomach.
- After coming back from your bathroom, set your lovely bed (or get the same done) where you had your last good night's sleep. Preferably, use a new bed sheet and a new pillow cover.
- Walk in an open area, preferably surrounded by flowers, a gentle breeze, and greenery, while matching the rhythm of the steps of your feet with that of hand clapping. After sufficient hand clapping, continue matching the rhythm with your breath.

Every morning, the energy we accumulate and the composure we regain help us maintain our meditative state throughout the day. We can deal with distractions and chaos better when our minds are stable.

****

Chapter 20: While doing exercises in the morning.

Run the positive thought through your mind that you are going to do a very important activity of the day that will help you maintain your body and mind's fitness.

Before starting your exercise, check:

- Whether your dress is comfortable.
- Whether you left at least a half-hour gap after eating some light and healthy food.
- Whether you have done some warm up for 5-10 minutes, before starting your exercises, so that the body parts do not become strained or sprained while doing the exercises.
- Whether your gym, hall, or lawn are tidy and clean,
- Whether the ground or the floor is plain.
- Whether the area is mosquito- and insect-free or if you have made arrangements to keep mosquitoes and insects from biting you.
- Whether you are away from the balcony or slope so that there is no chance of serious injury from an accidental fall while doing the exercises,
- Whether there is good air circulation in the room, hall, or lawn area that you have chosen to do your exercises.

- If there is enough space for you to move your hands and feet freely.
- Whether your exercise mat is clean, comfortable, and in good condition.
- If your mat is large enough or your lawn has good grass, you will not be injured if you fall while doing the exercises.
- Whether the front view from the place of exercise is

comfortable for you.

- Whether there is soothing background music playing or a natural calm environment with natural sounds like a breeze, falling leaves, and chirping or bird songs,

While doing your exercise, remain alert so that:

- You maintain a sufficient distance from the balcony or slope so that there is no chance of serious injury from an accidental fall.

- The good air circulation remains in the room, hall, or lawn area where you have chosen to do your exercises.
- Children or pets are away from you.
- Your phone remains in silent mode to avoid the tendency to answer a call.
- The background music remains on, at the place of your exercise or in a naturally calm environment.

Out of 24 hours every day, let's keep one hour exclusively reserved for the fitness exercise of the body and the mind, irrespective of how busy we may be.

That in turn helps increase the power of the mind in a big way, making us capable of remaining focused, cool, and stable, even in the face of external distractions.

****

REMAINING MEDITATIVE WHILE MAINTAINING AN IMPORTANT BALANCE IN LIFE

Chapter 21: To maintain the balance between your progress in life's goals and married life happiness.

You have your individual goal of life that you need to achieve: keeping your married life happiness intact. A focused effort is a must to maintain a balance between the two.

You might have met many married couples who are happy despite so many differences in thoughts, beliefs, and activities. You also might have met so many couples who got separated only because of very petty reasons due to impatience! There are so many cases of complete withdrawal from life's personal or professional goals due to strained marriages!

Run this thought through your mind: The happiness of your married life and the accomplishment of your personal goals will occur in tandem. Share this thought with your spouse.

You both may be ready to adjust many things to make both things grow together. Every day, talk to yourself in favor of the balanced growth of both aspects together.

Even though you and your spouse are both two individuals with different upbringings and ambitions, both can be in confluence by sacrificing their personal egos step by step, considering the latter as your biggest waste.

You both can often sit together in silence and may have the same first thought: you want to genuinely remain happy and at peace.

While sitting together, both of you will focus on setting or identifying your common goals. The discussion of your mutual interests will not involve any argument or fight, but will be a tried and true method of determining your common goals and joint strategy. Both spouses can work together to find a point of common ground. As a result, loads of unique individual goals become lighter. You will remain at ease as it becomes easier to handle the lesser-loaded individual tasks, as some activities will already be covered in the Common Zone.

Both of you will concentrate on making the best use of the 24 hours of the day to achieve your personal and family objectives.

Every person has 24 hours in a day. And by making the most of those 24 hours, many successful married people have made a name for themselves and demonstrated that life's goals and marital happiness can be achieved together. Things that are already proven by many can well be achieved by you, along with your spouse.

Methodical planning and positive mindsets by both spouses make a huge difference in the long run. You must rise far above the default perception levels during this process. And also, there will not be any question: "If it does not happen, then what?"

As you both need to run your family affairs together, there can be tentative schedules for your unique individual milestones based on the necessary engagements for both of you in your family. However, neither of you will take a halt on the matter of guarantee or surety, as both of you are already committed to achieving your goals and happiness.

Both of you will compromise for the sake of your family's happiness, but neither of you will ever entertain the thought of sacrificing your individual goals. To achieve life's goals and marital happiness, you must both remain internally strong.

If you cannot take up an opportunity because of your decision not to stay away from your family, then remain cool. Never be sad at the thought that you missed an opportunity. Both of you will run with the thought that you will get many opportunities without sacrificing your family's happiness and peace.

It is very important to focus on enhancing mutual compatibility between you and your spouse, which may be at the emotional, intellectual, or physical levels.

If you are short-tempered and are habitually fighting without logic and judgment, unlike your spouse, then the very next moment, take the pledge: "From today onwards, I will think twice before throwing rubbish words and sentences or before getting ready to fight with my spouse." If you run the thought at least once every morning, your family's happiness will gradually increase over time.

If you have the habit of putting all the blame on your spouse on every matter, then the very next moment, take the pledge: "From today onwards, instead of blaming my spouse on every matter, I will first check whether I am at fault. And even if she or he is at fault, I will give her or him the best counseling from my heart instead of playing the blame game."

If you have the habit of expressing doubts and fears on every single matter or while starting or doing an activity, then the very next moment, sit down comfortably and take the pledge: "From today onwards, I will always think and talk about winning and will act like a winner."

If you have a sense of intellectual superiority over your spouse, sit down comfortably and make the following pledge: "From today on, I will make my spouse understand in a simple language the useful matters that she or he found difficult to understand, for the better happiness of our family."

****

REMAINING MEDITATIVE WHILE DEALING WITH YOUR SPOUSE

53

Chapter 22: When your spouse irrationally suspects you.

You know that you are innocent. At the same time, it's true that your spouse has the freedom to suspect you, but it's also your responsibility to remove the suspicion from her or his mind as early as possible.

How do you do that?

She or he may have seen or heard something related to you directly or indirectly, for which she or he has made assumptions based on her perception or adopted somebody else's assumption as her own, due to a lack of clarity.

Once you, or someone else on your behalf, shed light on the aforementioned matter, her or his suspicions will be dispelled.

If you run the above positive thought in your mind, no irritation will be produced in your mind. Wish her or him the best from the bottom of your heart. In that positive state of mind, focus on the matters that have caused suspicion in her mind.

Accumulate all the points that will help to remove her or his doubts. The whole process should be completed as soon as possible, as the spread and undesirable growth of suspicion are very fast. You will be able to do so because the power of the truth is tremendous.

Keep on running the positive thought about your spouse's state of mind. Focus on the powerful points that you have accumulated so that all the points come to the fore, one by one. Speak with her or him right away to dispel all of her or his suspicions. If she or he is not ready to listen to what you have to say, just wait for the right moment, when she or he will become receptive to your points.

Give her or him enough opportunity to open up so that she or he can tell you everything about her or his doubts about you.

Let the light of truth dispel all of her or his suspicions.

When she or he realizes the futility of his or her suspicion, he or she will clear his or her mind of all negative thoughts. Hug her or him to show your appreciation for the good efforts.

If you are still unable to help her or him overcome their doubts, keep your positive thoughts in mind and continue to try sincerely. In the meantime, you may choose someone with a better meditative state to try on your behalf.

****

Chapter 23: Your spouse nags you frequently.

You may not have immediate control over her or his nagging behavior.

But:

You may practice remaining cool and wish her or him the best from your heart.

In that cool and composed mental state:

Believe that she or he has been nagging you or someone for a good cause, as if a jeweller has been trying to bring shine to a tarnished gold piece to convert it to a sparkling gold piece.

Forgive her every time she or he nags you so that no wasted thought about her or him can remain stagnant in your mind and bother you.

When you remain cool, irrespective of her or his nagging, the effect of nagging will wane. In that cool environment, listen attentively to every word she or he has uttered. Analyze and search for a solution. If at all possible, extend your hand and propose a mutually agreeable solution.

There may be some issues at your end that you can easily manage. If there are issues at her or his end or at both ends, propose discussing them with her or him, whenever she or he will become cool.

You should, in fact, feel good that there is someone to nag you all the time. Consider this: You are improving yourself day by day as a result of her or his nagging conversations. Take the remaining nagging conversations as a part of her or his diverse personality.

Your mind will remain happy and peaceful.

****

Chapter 24: When your spouse seeks divorce from you.

Respect the wish and the sentiment of your spouse in the matter of divorce, and run a positive thought in your mind about her or him. She or he has the right to seek, and may feel the need for, a break from you.

However, sometimes your spouse may abruptly take the decision to leave merely based on her or his temporary emotional state or due to some misunderstanding.

You need to have the determination to give your best effort to resolve the issue and retain the relationship if the issue has arisen due to a temporary emotional outbreak or misunderstanding.

Misunderstanding or false doubt is a major cause of divorce for either of the spouses.

But, should we allow something arbitrary to derail a loving and trusting relationship? Definitely not.

If, with all the considerations and good sense, your spouse is willing to depart from you, then give consent to that wish with happiness. Your happiness is due to the fact that you are making your spouse happier by departing with her or him as per her or his wish. Keep wishing her or him the best and keeping on helping her or him as and when required. If you have children, then you and your spouse may sit down to make the best plan for them that will work after your departure. You must respect the wishes of your children on the matter: under whose custody would each of your children love to be nurtured after your divorce?

This world is full of good people. If your spouse leaves you and you miss her or him terribly, you will have the positive thought in your head that you will undoubtedly meet another person who you will accept as your new spouse.

Constant goodwill toward your divorced spouse and the genuine hope of meeting a new life partner will, in turn, help you maintain your peace of mind.

****

REMAINING MEDITATIVE WHILE HANDLING SENSITIVE MATTERS

Chapter 25: One of your friends, relatives, or acquaintances shared sensitive personal information with you, but your mind has developed the tendency to pass on the information to somebody else.

It's the power of trust and confidence in you because of which your friend, relative, or acquaintance shared sensitive personal information with you. Her or his trust in you was such that you would keep the information confidential. You might be so sure of yourself that you can give her or him sound advice based on the information.

So, before speaking to anyone about a third person's personal matter, one of the best practices is to think deeply about what to say and what not to say. This is a daily requirement.

One usual tendency is that we tell other people's secrets to another person and then request that person not disclose them to a third person. This way, a secret matter becomes an open secret.

The usual notion is to reply to someone's query promptly and also to become an expert on many things. However, the smart way is to pause for a moment, take a deep breath, and ask your mind whether the sentence, phrase, or word you are about to share is someone's personal, sensitive information.

If you can keep your mind stable and cool through regular practice of remaining in the meditative state, then at any time of the day or night, while making any talk, you will be less likely to let your tongue slip. While talking, talk with full focus on every word you speak. No secret talk can easily come out of your mouth when the mind is stable, cool, and focused.

Even if some secret matter leaks accidentally, you must stop it as soon as you identify it. That is possible when you remain meditative. Because the usual notion is that once something comes out, either you feel the tendency to open up completely or the person in front of you convinces you to fully open up.

If you have the mastery of remaining in the meditative state all the time, you will be able to maintain good control in all of the aforesaid cases.

****

REMAINING MEDITATIVE WHILE HANDLING YOUR CHERISHED MOMENTS

Chapter 26: When you become an overnight star.

Remain stable, composed, and balanced so that the jerk of your sudden fame cannot confuse you or throw you off track.

You have just gotten a break, which is the biggest opportunity for you to sustain and grow. Run this thought through your mind: You have a bigger responsibility for your fans and followers.

Your stardom has just built a bigger platform for you. So, your sudden fame is actually a big beginning.

It's on you to decide how consistently and swiftly you would like to maintain the tempo.

Focus and act on your newly constructed platform. Your huge number of fans and followers will support and inspire you with big claps and loud shouts to keep you growing in a big way if they find you irresistible and unstoppable.

It is up to you to decide whether you will come and go like a big bubble or whether you will continue ascending and reach the summit.

Let your mind remain relaxed, positive, hopeful, and alert so that the quality and style of your actions, which have become hot favorites for so many people, can keep you standing apart from the rest.

The advantage and opportunity that your sudden fame has provided you should make you even more determined to see the sky as limitless. Take inspiration from your surroundings and go ahead with the tremendous energy that you have in you.

You don't have time to look back and mingle with the wasted thoughts and memories that will make you slower and weaker.

You cannot afford to give your ego any space in your heart.

Run this powerful thought through your mind: Your sudden fame has made you such a powerhouse that, through your creativity and good works, you can do wonders to bring happiness to the hearts of millions of people in the world.

****

Chapter 27: While celebrating your hard-earned success.

Run the best thought for everyone who has helped you succeed, both directly and indirectly.

Also, keep the best thought for all those who discouraged you and made fun of you, because of whom you took your path to success as a challenge and intensified your efforts.

While enjoying the celebration of your success, enjoy it with full spirit and joy, as that is the victory of your hard efforts, dedication, and smart plan.

Consider the celebration of every success of yours as a grand event, and keep this thought in your mind: every such celebration will encourage the aspirants of such success to make their efforts more focused and harder.

While celebrating, keep this in your mind all the time: "Let there be so many celebrations in the days to come, and let the next celebration be grander. Let every success represent the grandeur and glory of persistence and perseverance."

Through your celebration, let there be more happiness and peace in your mind.

Let your hard-earned success inspire many.

Through the celebration of your success, let many people learn more about your success story.

Make a commitment to continue doing your best to replicate your successes so that more and more people can be inspired by them.

****

REMAINING MEDITATIVE WHILE AT WORK OR AT HOME

Chapter 28: Calming down and relaxing in a scheduled way while doing your work.

Calming down and relaxing in between tasks, as dictated by your flexible schedule, is a great way to stay healthy and active. That in turn can keep your mind happy and cool.

Schedule short breaks between tasks to maintain work momentum. Allow your body and mind to rejuvenate during those brief periods of rest.

During every short break, apply the appropriate relaxation techniques for your body and mind.

At your workplace, try for a warm-up of 5 minutes in every 90 minutes of work.

In the morning, at home, let there be a daily warm-up and meditation for at least one hour.

Every weakened, at least once, take your mind to your childhood, for some time, to release your stresses and come back relaxed.

You may apply the golden rule: When your concentration starts deviating when your eyes are strained and there is an urge or signal from your brain for a break, just take a break. Get rejuvenated and come back to work with full energy.

After returning home from work in the evening, 5–10 minutes of lying down after completely loosening the hands and legs will relax your body and mind.

Before going to sleep at night, 10 minutes of sleep meditation will make your mind ready for a sound sleep.

Find ways to give relaxation to your body and mind on various occasions:

- If you are on a manufacturing shop floor, move away from the machine area and find a location away from an electrical panel or hazardous substance that does not obstruct the movement of others or the flow of materials.

- If you are in a paddy field, take advantage of the green grass.
- And, if you are on a long drive, take a halt at a safe location, get out of the vehicle, utilize the nearby open space, or park.

When you are busy, you may calm down and relax at regular intervals.

You can relax your body and mind in your own way during short breaks while doing long-duration work, such as by following the following proven steps:

- Wash your hands using a hand soap.
- Wash your face.
- Splash clean water in both eyes—at least 20 times in each eye.
- Choose a location that allows for free limb movement and air circulation.
- Rub both palms vigorously and keep the warm palms on both eyes.
- Move and rotate your hands, wrists, and fingers.
- While taking deep breaths, stretch out both hands and look at the sky or roof. Return to your normal position while exhaling deeply.
- Move your legs, rotate your ankles, stretch up on your toes, and come back; move your knees up and down.
- Slowly rotate your waist on both sides alternately.
- Move your head up and down slowly and steadily.
- Slowly and steadily turn your head to the left and right.
- Go back to work.

Relax with your passion:

Spend every evening and every weekend with your passion; it may be drawing and painting, spending time in the kitchen preparing your favorite dish, singing your favorite song, or dancing with your spouse, children, and friends.

Punch out your stresses:

You may have a boxing kit with a punch. Whenever you feel tense, make a number of punches to punch out your stresses.

When you can remain in the meditative state, you will be able to remain happy and relaxed throughout the day, even while doing your work.

****

Chapter 29: After you reach home from your work.

As soon as you reach home, leave all your work worries and memories behind and enter the world of your family. Run this positive thought that you have come back to a place where there is lots of peace and love, and your presence will make the environment livelier.

Take rhythmic steps as you walk to your house. Check the floor for water or oil spills, as well as broken glass pieces, to avoid slipping and injuring yourself.

Remember that you will not bring garbage thoughts into your home. Along with that, you will be careful not to bring trash, dirt, or viruses into your home.

Maintain the provision and habit of leaving shoes on the shoe rack and a sanitization shower or, at the very least, a hand sanitization facility at the front door.

With all positivity and an open heart, greet your spouse, children, and other members of your family, forgetting your tiredness.

Keep your old dress, office bag, and Tiffin-box in the proper places. (This will prevent your spouse from nagging you about it.)

While keeping your old dress in its place, decide on the outfit you will wear to work tomorrow or the next working day.(This is to ensure that your arrival at work is not delayed.)

While keeping your old clothes at the designated place, check whether you need to keep some clothes near the washing machine for washing.

Find a clean set of underwear and a handkerchief for tomorrow.

Make your alternative arrangement ready in your mind, in case you have forgotten anything that your spouse or children asked you to bring home.

Make your alternative, achievable plan for the evening ready if you could not take leave today, despite the fact that it was your spouse's birthday or your anniversary day and you badly forgot to carry something special while coming back home.

After being away for so many hours, there will be a natural instinct in your mind to hug your spouse or children. But, as much as you love them, go to the bathroom and freshen up before you hug them. Apply a light deodorant to your body, especially at your armpits, and change your dress.

After hugging and kissing your parents, spouse, children, and other members of your family, you may need to give your body five minutes to get energized and recharged for the remaining hours of the evening. Just lie down in your bed for five minutes, with your face up; open up your hands and legs; loosen those completely; keep your eyes closed; bring the wide, clear sky into your imagination. Take a deep breath slowly, in this position, at least five times.

After getting relaxed, divide the remaining hours of your evening with useful activities like spending some quality time with your children and spouse; making phone calls to your dear ones; going to the gym or exercising; and most importantly, pursuing your passion. This you will do every day, fresh, depending on the situation, even though you already may have a daily activity chart.

Before going to bed, take 10 minutes to reflect on the good things you did throughout the day, as well as the lessons you learned from any mistakes you made today.

Maintaining a meditative state at all times allows you to keep your mind stable and cool, allowing you to better concentrate on your various tasks, both personal and professional.

****

REMAINING MEDITATIVE WHILE DEALING WITH YOUR FEELINGS/ THOUGHTS/ EMOTIONS

Chapter 30: When your love proposal is rejected by the person you really love.

When you start loving someone, just love with the positive thought of sprouting happiness in his or her heart. That thought will make you happy. While making a love proposal to someone, almost everyone will expect love in return. But if you want to remain happy, try to love with the least expectation of return so that you do not become upset if he or she rejects your love.

If you can remain meditative, then you can keep yourself ready not to get hurt in matters of love. You may feel love for anyone, and you have the full right to love anyone.

If your personality, approach, and attitude can create love in her or his heart for you, then that will be great. But if your proposal is rejected by her or him, keep on loving and wishing silently.

Another important point is that love, in the long run, is positively infectious. A sunny day will come when the warmth of your innocent love will definitely touch the heart of your beloved. If you continue to love and nurture a flowering plant with a positive thought, the flowers will become glossier and more fragrant. This is a timeless, universal truth.

Run the thought through your mind that the rejection of your love proposal is not a matter of concern for you. So, while proposing, propose with full innocence—no demand, no repetition, no expectation. In that case, you will remain happy irrespective of the result.

If the person adversely reacts or misbehaves toward you in reply to your proposal, simply remain cool and honestly say "Sorry," but never repeat the proposal. Rather, consider her or his proposal as a gift from her or him. Sit down or lie down coolly without complaining to anyone about your failure.

Run this positive thought through your mind: the right time has come for you to take up the challenge of enhancing your worth and stature to great heights.

****

Chapter 31: When you lose your temper.

Sometimes a situation may arise when you lose your temper. But it makes the situation better if you think and verify whether the anger was because of some misunderstanding in your mind or due to some petty cause with negligible impacts that could have been easily ignored.

Irrespective of whatever may be the cause, run this thought through your mind: You are going to win over your temper so that it cannot cause more harm to your body and mind and also to others.

Look at the earth below you and the greenery around you, and think how magnificently those are maintaining calm despite so much embarrassment caused to them.

Every day, in the morning, fill your mind with as much positivity as possible. Let's try to avoid, as much as possible, irritating stories, news, and talks, especially in the morning. Throughout the day, you may face situations or get news that is stressful, undesirable, or annoying. However, if you regularly feed your mind healthy mental food such as motivational talks, meditation, or soothing music in the morning, you are less likely to lose your temper. If you can delay your temper, then you will gain better control over your mind.

The cause of the majority of anger is trivial. So, if you can run deep thought to find the root of anger, the likelihood of such anger recurring is reduced.

If the cause is somebody else's fault, then run the positive thought of diverting such thoughts in a constructive way. If you are angry with someone, instead of wasting time fighting or scolding, take on a large task by accepting the enormous challenge of completing the task.

****

Chapter 32: While cracking a joke.

You have a great sense of humor. You love and enjoy cracking jokes on every single occasion, irrespective of where you are. That, in fact, is your great creativity, as you have the ability to bring a smile to someone's face, making that face more beautiful.

Let every joke you crack make you happier. When you are happier, then you can spread that happiness to all those around you.

Even though you can crack a joke with spontaneity, it will be great if you could allow every word to pass through your internal filter. So, even if you act too quickly, your mind will be fully alert to ensure that the words you are about to release are with good intentions and will not create the tendency to make fun of someone's personality or trait.

Even after exercising the aforesaid filter, you will be able to exercise tremendous freedom in cracking jokes without hurting others.

If someone becomes enraged while you're making a joke, stay alert and immediately apologize for hurting her or his feelings.

It's quite normal that the words, sentences, or plot that you used to crack a joke may hurt someone's feelings. Because those may not be appropriate at that time when that person's mood is off.

It is always preferable to conduct a self-analysis of the words or sentences spoken. If you still believe you did not say or mean anything negative, express your conviction to the person in question.

When people love your jokes, but you suddenly catch an unexpected "hurt feeling" in someone's mind, remain calm and take the event as a lesson to learn. Every such jerk gives you an opportunity to improve your skill at cracking jokes as well as the quality of your jokes.

****

REMAINING MEDITATIVE WHILE HANDLING SPECIAL OCCASIONS AND SITUATIONS

Chapter 33: While delivering a public speech.

Before starting the speech, you should feel better with the thought that you are going to deliver a great public speech. In fact, you are an expert in the concerned subject matter, by dint of which you are invited to deliver a speech.

In the case of informal private talk or brainstorming sessions, you can say whatever you want without thinking too hard, because the goal is either informal communication or the exchange of rough ideas.

But, before delivering a public speech, thorough preparation is of the utmost importance.

Run this strong thought through your mind: You are going to deliver the best ever speech in front of so many great audiences in a majestic way. That continuous thought will inspire you to make a smarter plan for action for your forthcoming speech event.

Preparation for a public speaking event includes not only the content of the speech but also your outfit, shoes, and hairstyle; how you approach the stage, your walking pattern and standing pause; how you hold the phone; how you begin and conclude your speech; how you crack relevant jokes and cite appropriate examples; and many other factors.

The most important preparation, however, is to practice remaining happy and at peace while remaining firm and in control during a public speech. 90% of your success in a public speech will come from that, because when there is a flow of happiness in your mind, when you are maintaining peace, and when your words and sentences are under your full control, you can deliver an awesome speech, impromptu, on your subject.

****

Chapter 34: While facing a media interview.

Whatever the purpose of a media interview, feel good that you have an opportunity to express yourself. So, keep calm and express everything that adds value.

Maintain your resolve to speak only about the positives and ignore the negatives.

Focus on each word before delivering.

A uniform flow of genuine happiness will be radiated from your face during your interview. A high level of confidence and clarity will make your sentences lovely and beautiful for the audience.

There will be no controversial or negative talk, no blaming, no wild guessing, and no assumptions. There will be no ambiguous statements or boasting.

Once spoken or delivered, words or sentences cannot be taken back or undone. So, prior to making any revelation in the media, speak only those things that are ethical, logical, rational, appropriate, factual, and soothing. Do self-talk and analysis quickly, not only before the interview but also at each stage of speaking in the media.

Let's not talk just for the sake of speaking. Unless you are sure of the authenticity of a word or sentence, it is always better to keep quiet.

All the aforesaid temperaments and courses of action will be possible prior to, during, and after a media interview, making the interview a grand one if you are in the meditative stage, in which you will be focused, cool, stable-minded, and in a happy state. In that state of mind, neither hesitation nor confusion can cause your words or sentences to become distorted or deviate from the perfection and clarity to which you aspire and cherish.

****

Chapter 35: While appearing in an examination.

Every examination that you are going to appear in is a golden opportunity for you to truly make yourself glitter. You have taken up the challenge that you are going to make yourself ready for the examination and will put in as much effort as you can.

But the most important thing is honesty in your efforts to develop a love for the examinations.

The eagles love to play in the sky with the storm, whereas the other birds are very scared of the storm. The reason is that the eagles are confident in their abilities and so can relax and go up and down with the help of the storm.

If you can run this positive thought continuously in your mind that examinations or tests are going to help you get elevated, then you can play with every examination brilliantly, as the eagles do with the storms.

Eventually, this thought will be ingrained in your mind: that there is an examination every day, both of your surroundings and of yourself. As soon as that thought and belief become deeply rooted, from that point on, you will accept every examination with a spirit similar to that of winning in sports and will genuinely remain happy whether you win or not. Participating wholeheartedly will be enjoyable and an important part of your life.

****

Chapter 36: While doing an important job.

Irrespective of whether the job is interesting for you or not, you need to focus.

The brain surgeon cannot afford to have his or her mind diverted even for a moment in the operating room; the pilot cannot afford to have his or her mind diverted while flying in a turbulent path in extremely bad weather; the singer cannot afford to have his or her focus broken on a big stage in front of 100,000 audience members; and the driver cannot afford to get distracted while transporting some serious patients to the emergency section of a hospital. Those are a few of many examples.

You need to focus, act, and achieve, and continue to remain that way. When you can focus while working, irrespective of the situation, with an uninterrupted flow of happiness in the mind, you actually go to the meditative state.

How do you do that?

Develop a love for the work you are going to do.

It's great if you can get work done on the topic of your great passion. In such a case, distortion cannot stop you from performing, and your intuition will help you take the required lead as the work progresses.

Otherwise,

Look at something really big like the wide-open sky, a sea, or a green or colorful field; take a deep breath at least twice; and then make a list of the points for yourself in a notebook or in your mind that will increase your interest in the work.

Physical and mental preparation while starting the work.

- It's good if the place of your work and the device you are working with are perfectly neat and clean.

Otherwise,

With a duster, clean the table and chair, the slab, and your device, e.g., your laptop, before starting the work.

- Sit or stand comfortably so that you can do the work comfortably.
- Visualize the benefits that you and/or others are going to get if the work is accomplished.
- If possible, play soft and soothing background music at a low volume and leave it alone.

while you are in the midst of your work.

- Remain straight whether you are working in a sitting, standing, or lying position. If you need to work in the leaning pause or with your head up, then you will come back straight at regular intervals and remain there for some time.
- At regular intervals, take deep breaths so that you feel at ease.

****

Chapter 37: When you are in an important meeting (personal or official).

It's required to focus on the subject matter of the meeting. Let's not say anything for the sake of saying something.

If your thoughts revolve around the topic of discussion and your attention is on what others are saying in the meeting, then you will be able to filter your words, phrases, and sentences before speaking.

To focus on the topic and the discussion, your eyes and ears will have to be purely on the group of people attending the meeting.

Maintain your cool and gently hold your points whenever it is your turn. While understanding, analyzing, and replying, simply follow these steps:

Silently observe which way the meeting is going.

If you are not able to contribute, or if there is nothing to say, then it's better to maintain silence.

Silence is many times better than speaking nonsense.

Let's make our internal filter system so strong that non-value-added thoughts and talks can be totally eliminated from the meeting.

****

Chapter 38: While finalizing an important deal.

You need to pay full attention while finalizing a deal so that each term and condition related to the deal may be looked into thoroughly and understood.

You are going to do a very important task that may be a combination of a number of interlinked sub-tasks. You need to understand the required as well as the comfortable points of the deal documents.

Before agreeing and signing any document, you need to sit comfortably and read each and every page of the contract document.

Let's not be in a hurry. Reading the documents may be completed in a single go or in many goes, but it's required to clarify the doubts. So making notes of the queries is important. The majority of legal complications arise when we sign a deal after a half-hearted read. Many surprises occur afterward.

If the deal is related to a project or an assignment, it is required to understand the feasibility, deadline, and input information. If the deal is related to a property, it's required to understand its authenticity and worth.

If you have deputed or given authority to someone to go through the deal documents on your behalf, then you need to double-check how trustworthy and capable the person is.

You will keep a positive attitude about the deal.

****

Chapter 39: While adopting, initiating, and sustaining the best practices.

You will run on the positive thought that you will adopt or initiate some of the best practices for you as well as for others, with the purpose of having a better life as well as helping others to have better lives.

Whatever best practices you have adopted or initiated, you will let them sustain themselves and keep growing. For example, suppose you have started the monthly drive for tree planting in and around your area and have started educating people on its benefits. Once you start with a positive approach, you will continue doing the same and will involve more and more people for the betterment of the environment.

Let's look into the following:

While raising immunity awareness:

Consider this: You will conduct as many immune-related studies as possible with great enthusiasm and love! As per the thought, while searching for the best foods and the best exercises, you will focus on the term "Immunity" so that your search and your intakes can remain within and around the topic.

While prioritizing your physical and mental health:

Every day, you will run this thought through your mind: "Your physical and mental health are the top priorities for maintaining your professional, family, and social lives." That thought will motivate you to devote some quality time daily for meditation and a series of physical exercises, including breathing exercises.

With persistence, you will be able to escape the usual tag: "Busy at Work, No Time for Exercise." Keep this thought in your mind: how important it is to calm down and relax in a scheduled way to keep the brain and body healthy and active.

Allotting some more quality time for your family:

You are busy with your work. But your spouse, children, parents, and elders are so important to you!

You can simply enhance some more quality time for each of your family members by analyzing your various engagements over the course of 24 hours. If required, you will have to run such an analysis again and again.

Avoiding Gossip:

Your mind can clearly distinguish between "Gossip" and "A healthy discussion." Every morning, you will have this thought: In the whole day, you will not get yourself involved in any such conversation group where the subjects are related to how Mr. M yawns or how big Mr. N's belly is or how funny the talks of Mr. Q are because of his stammering problem, etc., etc. Keep an eye on how the time saved by not gossiping can be put to good use in some constructive thoughts and works.

Resorting to Better Hygiene:

Take the pledge not to let harmful microorganisms enter your body. So, thorough washing or sanitization of your hands and other body parts, every time you feel the need, will be one of your prime habits.

Adopting or initiating a better way of greeting:

While greeting someone, greet them with all the enthusiasm that you possess so that that person gets enriched by the spark of your enthusiasm and positivity, which in turn will multiply your own enthusiasm and happiness. Every skill and every work that is directly or indirectly meant to serve the human being and nature is respectable. So everyone deserves high regard from you.

Nullifying your ego and helping others do the same:

Take your mind to the virtual world of the universe's millions of diverse activities and see where you stand. Do this exercise daily when you feel egoistic about your status, irrespective of whether it is professional, financial, personal, or social.

Nurture your passions:

When you are in the midst of an activity that is your passion, you will observe how much happiness and joy you experience inside of you, even though the work may be hard and time-consuming. Others may not get the actual feeling of your happiness.

So, the more you nurture your passions to grow, the more you will be happy and at peace.

Looking at life from a broader perspective:

Whenever you get a chance, sit down under the wide sky and look around you. Imagine who you are and what your purpose and utilities are in this world. Such imagination, in the long run, will bring a broader perspective to the fore for the betterment of everyone.

****

REMAINING MEDITATIVE WHILE DEALING WITH YOUR FOOD

Chapter 40: While taking mental food.

Around you, you will find mental food everywhere. But you need to keep yourself alert so that you take only the food that is edible to you.

For example, if you have seen someone rise in business by engaging in foul play, you will not adopt that trick.

Let us cultivate the deeply ingrained belief that nature is an infinitely open book from which you can obtain as many useful inputs as you require.

Let the open sky teach us to be as broad as we need to be; let the great earth teach us to be as tolerant as we need to be; let the magnificent lotus in the dirty mud teach us to be as adjustable as we need to be.

Let the balanced co-existence of the beautiful scenes, colors, designs, diversity, depth, perfection, and natural fragrances in nature teach us how limitless and diverse we can be in our levels of achievements in a balanced way.

Let's learn how strongly an eagle focuses to catch its prey. Also, elephants travel in groups, guarding their calves along the way. Let us learn from the ants how to work together to transport a heavy item over a long distance.

Let's spend some quality time every day with serene nature. That will undoubtedly increase happiness and peace of mind, as well as provide us with mental nourishment.

****

Chapter 41: While taking food.

Let the following thought run through your mind: "I am going to have the food that will bring peace to my heart." You will have that thought irrespective of whether you are at home, in a restaurant, or at a party.

Focusing on checkpoints similar to the following may be useful:

- Have you planned in such a way that there is a gap of around half an hour after you complete your last exercise? (This gives your body time to normalize.)
- Are you hungry, or have you just sat down to keep someone company? (Because if you eat without getting hungry, you may develop digestive issues.)
- Have you thoroughly washed your hands? Otherwise, harmful microorganisms may be transmitted to your food from your hands.
- Are the utensils clean, or are small bits of previously consumed food particles or dishwashing soap present?
- Are you sitting in a comfortable position while eating? This is because standing puts more pressure on your intestines. If you are in a sleeping position, there is a chance that food may enter your windpipe, causing a serious medical emergency.
- Have you gone over your restricted food list in case you have any health problems? (If you do not follow that list, your health may suffer.)
- Have you taken the medicine that you need to take before food?
- Have you noticed any abnormal smells or tastes in the food? (The food may not be freshly prepared, or while preparing or keeping it without a lid, some undesirable item may fall into the food or it may be over-burnt.)
- Have you just drank a glass of water and then started eating

without pausing? (There may be a digestive problem if you do not keep a gap between drinking water and taking solid food.)

- Have you kept a glass of drinking water nearby while eating so that if the food is dry or if some food gets stuck in your food pipe or neck by accident, sips of water can provide good relief?

- Are your lips full of lipsticks or lip gloss while taking food? (For ladies): Unless they are made of health-friendly materials, those cosmetics may cause long-term health problems.

- Is the food combination correct? (A dietician or a health specialist may suggest the correct combination.)

- Is there enough light while eating so that you can easily see if there are any foreign particles? (An unintentional fall of the cook's hair, a fly or insect, etc.)

- Have you kept your bowl or dish with food away from the edges of the table? Consider yourself hungry, and your delectable food falling to the ground because you took your dish or bowl just at the edge of your table.

- Have you ever used a food towel to cover your pants when you're sitting and eating? (It is too awkward if you discover food particles or stains in your trousers later on, in a public place.)

- Have you eaten while driving? (That may divert your attention, increasing the chance of road accidents.)

- Have you eaten in such a hurry that food is not properly ground in your mouth, causing digestion issues?

- Have you said "thank you" to the person who has prepared such delicious food for you?

- Have you said "thank you" to the Almighty for giving you such a lovely tongue to enjoy the food?

- Have you taken only as much food as you need so that there is no food waste in your dish or bowl?

- Have you taken the food in silence or in light conversation? (If you are over-excited while talking, talk continuously, or smile heavily, food may make the wrong entry into your windpipe, causing a medical emergency.)

- While going to get food, have you discovered that someone near you needs the food more than you do? If so, please offer him or her, your food. You will really get mental peace if you can feed a person who is starving.

****

Chapter 42: While preparing the special food for your very special guest.

"I am going to prepare the best food that will be loved by our very special guest."

- Collect first-hand information about the favorite choices of the guest.
- Run this thought through your mind again and again. Your mind should feel the taste and aroma of the food before preparing it.
- While thoroughly washing your face and hands, as well as wearing a clean cloth and apron, think about this and remind yourself that no germ can enter the food at any stage.
- With best wishes, inspect all raw food components, carefully wash them, and place them easily accessible for preparation.
- Prepare the food with extreme care. During the cooking process, your mind will be preoccupied with how pure, delicious, and healthy the food will be. Water will be very clean and fresh, and salt and sugar quantities will be measured by your mind and be neither more nor less. Oil and spices will be appropriate. The flame used to prepare the food will be neither the maximum nor the minimum.
- Food will neither be too raw nor overcooked. The care and focus will be such that no food will be burned while preparing.
- While serving the special food to your special guest, keep the best positive thought in mind that the guest will enjoy and digest the food easily. While serving, fully focus on that thought.

****

REMAINING MEDITATIVE WHILE DEALING WITH YOUR SLEEP

Chapter 43: When you are not able to sleep at night.

When your mind becomes unstable momentarily, you may not be able to sleep at night.

Run the positive thought in your mind that you will soon be able to have sound sleep every night.

The first thing that can be done is to sit down and fill up a chart of interesting and useful activities for all 24 hours of the day, for all the days of every week, so that your body and mind, including your brain, can get fully engaged in useful activities.

That way, every day, from the morning until the late evening, you will remain fully packed with a number of valuable and interesting activities. Also, when all 24 hours of the day are occupied with activities, there will not be any time for getting stressed with negative news and thoughts.

After doing all the scheduled activities throughout the day and the evening, your brain, along with the other parts of your body, will get tired. Also, during the whole day, you will not feed any negative data to your mind in the form of news of crimes, chaos, murder, brutality, social and political disturbance, etc. In fact, you will not be able to spare any time for useless events or programs. So, throughout the day, your mind will remain busy with useful thoughts.

Sit down at regular intervals in deep silence to make your mind stable and cool. When you are tired after a long day of good work and your mind is stable, lie down in bed after drinking a glass of warm water and relaxing your hands and feet. Listen to something soothing and gentle (preferably sleep music). Without your knowledge, you will be in a deep and peaceful sleep.

****

Chapter 44: When you suddenly wake up at midnight.

Assume you had a dream of riding a wild horse or being chased by a tiger. Or suppose there was a sudden, unexpected sound.

You suddenly woke up, keeping your mid-night dream incomplete.

Lie down straight, with your face up; simply take your hands and feet in completely loose and relaxed positions, and then do deep breathing, very slowly and steadily, for at least five times. Try to reconstruct the dream with a positive ending.

In that lying position, rotate your body slowly to the left side and, with the help of your hands, slowly come to the sitting position.

Sit comfortably for a few minutes in a relaxed posture to allow your body to relax.

Slowly take a glass of warm water.

Now, ask yourself:

- Did you miss something before going to bed last night, because of which you are feeling uneasy? (Run this thought in your mind: "You are going to make up, whatever you missed last night and will rather perform better, at the earliest.")
- Did you think junk last night, because of which the horizon of your mind became vague, resulting in interrupted sleep? This world is wide. The scope of doing big has become wider with time. So, there is no room for junk. (Run this thought through with full determination.)
- Did you eat junk food last night, because of which your digestive system is disturbed? There are so many delicious and natural foods to eat, enjoy, and be at peace with in the world. Take a pledge to resort to food with nature's goodness. Take baking soda, ginger, or another appropriate item to help with your upset stomach.

- Has somebody's bad words or undesirable deeds have hurt you, because of which your sleep is interrupted? (The golden rule is to forget all the bad words and deeds as fast as possible and forgive those who uttered those bad words and committed those bad deeds.)
- Has depression become deeply rooted in you due to some recent failure or incident? (Take a thick sheet of paper and write down the much-desired target that you love to beat. (Put that sheet in front of you.)
- Has a near-term goal that you want to achieve caused the interrupted sleep? (Do some more work related to your dream, even though it's midnight. You will feel happy with the thought that you have spent your midnight oil to fulfill your cherished dream.)

Sleep again whenever you feel sleepy, with the positive thought that you will get up in the morning with more positive energy.

Lie down again with your eyes closed and body relaxed and run the deep thought of how the world is in a sound sleep. Let there be very soothing sleep meditation music. Relax and get ready again for a sound sleep.

You will fall asleep soon.

****

Chapter 45: While going to sleep.

While going to sleep, keep this thought in your mind: You are going to rejuvenate your body mind together. The sleep will be magnificent for you regardless of the duration or location. Such wholehearted thought will undoubtedly aid your sleep and bring you peace of mind.

Checkpoints similar to the following may be helpful for you:

- Have you started chatting with someone or allowed someone to initiate a chat with you before going to sleep? (You never know how long the chat will continue, badly breaking your sleep schedule.)

- Have you kept a soft carpet or a floor mat near the open edge of your bed? (So that, in case of an accidental fall during sleep, during a lovely dream of catching something, you do not suffer from a serious injury.)

- Did you want to start ironing your clothes when you were sleepy, before going to sleep? You never know when you'll unintentionally fall asleep. Imagine what will happen to your iron and cloth.)

- Have you kept yourself away from horror photos, videos, and stories before going to sleep? (Because those may keep you awake all night.)

- Have you checked whether the setting of your alarm clock is undesirable to you? (That may spoil your early morning's sweet sleep.)

- Have you started reading a heavy book while lying on the bed? (The book may fall on your chest and remain there if you fall asleep unintentionally, inviting the risk of a serious health emergency.)

- Have you brushed your teeth thoroughly before going to sleep? (So that the next morning, people do not have to run away from you, due to bad breath.)

- Are your bladder and rectum empty before you go to sleep?
- Have you started cooking something when you are sleepy and left your kitchen just to lie down for five minutes? You never know when you'll fall asleep. Imagine what can happen in the kitchen.)
- Is your dress loose and stretchy? (So that, during your sleep, you can breathe easily and blood circulation in the body can be uninterrupted.)
- Have you taken your post-dinner medicine?
- Have you chosen your appropriate pillow before going to sleep?
- Have you double-checked whether your front and back doors are locked? (So that undesirable, uninvited guests can't enter your house when you are all in deep sleep.)
- Have you double-checked whether you have closed your gas stove? (So that a dangerous surprise can't happen when you are in deep sleep.)
- Have you avoided eating acidic foods before going to bed? (So that you do not have to suffer at night due to broken sleep caused by acidity.)
- Before sleeping, have you kept your mobile phone away from your bed? (In order to avoid some high-risk accidents caused by mobile phones.)
- Have you kept the volume of your phone's messages on mute? (So that you do not get disturbed due to late-night messages.)
- Have you continued listening to some music or a discussion using your earphones in a lying or sitting position while putting your phone on charge before going to sleep? (You never know when you will fall asleep, putting you at high risk.)
- Have you kept yourself from going to your balcony when you

are sleepy?

- Have you finished smoking when you are sleepy? (This prevents the clothes in the room from catching fire if you go to sleep with incomplete smoking.)
- Have you allowed your pet to play near you before you go to sleep? (Your sleep may be badly hampered.)
- Have you kept your room heater on before going to sleep with your room's air circulation and ventilation completely off, increasing the risk of death?
- Have you kept your laptop or desktop in sleep mode before going to sleep?
- Have you made your bed with a clean bed sheet and a nice blanket?
- Have you made plans for the next day before going to bed?
- Before going to sleep, have you calmed down your body and mind to bring down your stress level by taking slow walks for 5–10 minutes, followed by comfortable sitting for some time, followed by a relaxed lie-down?
- Have you taken a glass of warm water before going to sleep? (So that your body can remain hydrated and food particles from your food pipe can go down, facilitating better digestion.)
- Have you said good night to your dear ones before going to sleep? (As every night may be the last night for anyone.)
- Have you cleared your mind of your hatred or anger toward someone before going to bed so that you can sleep soundly?

****

REMAINING MEDITATIVE TO FACILITATE YOUR SYNCHRONIZATION WITH NATURE

Chapter 46: Your synchronization with the Mother Nature.

Nature is with so much goodness. So, we can try to gain knowledge & learn discipline from her.

The best approach will be to try to synchronize with Mother Nature.

Synchronize with her to soothe your body and the mind.

You need to manage to spend some quality time every day, with Nature.

You may have a garden of health-friendly plants and grass, in and around your house. And, if you sit at the balcony or near your window and spend some time, every day, enjoying the Natural views of the surroundings, then that may help to calm both the body and mind. Especially, relaxing the eyes with the pleasant views, pleasing the ears with the natural sounds, and soothing the whole body with the natural breeze. With every rejuvenating act, you get your mind refreshed and enhance happiness.

If it's not convenient for you to look at the natural beauty from the window or from the balcony or to build a garden near you, then at least, you can look at the hard or soft photos or videos of Nature's grandeur, as and when you can. That will also help to calm down your mind. And also, if it is not convenient for you to listen to the natural sound of Nature, then listen to the recorded relevant audios or videos, to have some soothing effects on your mind.

Every morning, do meditation for some time, taking the green grass, wide blue sky, or big waves of the sea, as the background in the mind. Because, if you bring the natural background in the mind, Nature will make you relaxed and energized, greatly. You may try this with immediate effect, as like many, this one is a proven fact.

Divide your works into suitable slots and fill up the gaps between every two slots to get nearness to Nature, as far as possible. At the end of every slot, you may get the opportunity to take a halt for a few minutes and enjoy Nature's beauty.

Flowers are so beautiful and pleasing! Just enjoy from the heart, the beauty of so many flowers, so many colors, sizes, shapes, and fragrances, without touching & plucking. For better mental happiness and peace, stop the practice of the ruthless plucking of innocent flowers.

Fill the surroundings, with more & more greenery.

Wholeheartedly enjoy the soothing music of Nature, contributed by the twittering birds, cool breeze, and tree leaves.

Have a Natural Sleep, every night.

Stay away from the sleeping medicine, as far as possible. Rather, before going to sleep at night, feel the original sleeping music from Nature or recorded sleeping music audio.

Discover peace all the time whenever you are with Nature.

Enhance your happiness by discovering various standing, sitting, twisting, bending, inverted, and balancing postures in Nature. You may get surprised to find various natural health postures, all around, in Nature that you can follow for your better health.

Get yourself nurtured, Natural Way.

Let the brain gets developed, natural way. Let the happiness accumulated in you from the beauty of Nature helps to release the happy chemicals in the brain, in a balanced way.

Let the natural detoxification takes place in our body and the mind, as far as possible.

Let the rivers flow with clean water and let there be abundant growth of trees, at the banks of the rivers.

Live mainly on natural Food.

Remain to feel good by keeping a balance between the alkaline and the acidic foods.

Utilize the power of silence, just like the serenity of Nature. The best creativity can get nourished, in such a state.

Understand the Law of Nature and pledge not to act against the same.

Remain in the green space, as far as possible. Create the aura of the green space around you, so that you can get the best out of the goodness of Mother Nature.

Everyone can learn from Mother Nature, how to love unconditionally and become happier.

Feel young & dynamic and take inspiration from the ever young & dynamic Nature. You will understand how soothing such a feeling is!

****

REMAINING MEDITATIVE WHEN YOU ARE INSIDE YOUR BATHROOM

Chapter 47: When you are inside your bathroom.

You've gone into the bathroom to freshen up. So, feel good about the same, irrespective of whether you are emptying your bowels or bladder, taking a bath, flashing water in your eyes, or brushing your teeth. In one sentence, you can say that you are in the process of cleaning your body.

When you clean up your body, think about sweeping and mopping your mind as well. From the time of making entry to the bathroom until coming out of the same, checkpoints similar to the following may help you get better results:

While entering the bathroom, check:

- Whether the floor is slippery,
- Whether you have worn a suitable bathroom slipper,
- Whether or not the trash in the trash can was removed today,
- Whether there is any leakage or water clogging in the bathroom,
- Whether the bathroom seat is properly fastened so that while sitting on it, there is no chance of an accident,
- Whether the geyser is of the gas type that can cause suffocation inside the bathroom,
- While still inside the bathroom, ensure that the toilet has been thoroughly flushed and that the toilet seat has been thoroughly cleaned before and after use,
- Whether you thoroughly cleaned your hands after using the toilet with a hand wash and hand sanitizer.

While leaving the bathroom, check:

- Whether you have closed your washbasin valve or other valves.
- Whether you have switched off the lights, exhaust, etc.

- Whether you have closed your bathroom door.

After leaving the bathroom, remind yourself that you have freshened up and are now ready for the day's many exciting activities!

Your positive thoughts and focus while entering, staying in, and leaving your bathroom will keep your body and mind fresh all day long.

****

Remaining Meditative WHEN YOU ARE ON YOUR TRIP

Chapter 48: While getting ready before going out from home for a trip.

Generally, you may approach the matter of your trip in a casual way, but later on, on the way, you may face lots of problems. So, it's required to bring the mind to a calm state and focus on the preparation for the whole trip.

Visualization of each and every step before starting the trip helps a lot. Imagine how easy and entertaining the trip can be. Imagine how handy your comprehensive list of actions is going to be in making the whole trip enjoyable for you and/or your family.

Keep sufficient time on hand for the preparation. Whether the trip is for personal or professional reasons, you should be pleased with it.Remain happy with the feeling that the trip is bringing new opportunities for you to get exposure to a new environment, new scenery, new faces, new experiences and learning, and new enjoyment.

Your smart checklist will make your preparation interesting. You will check to see whether:

- Your detailed travel plan is completed.
- All the in-and-out payment options that may be required during the trip are updated and active.
- All the required ID proofs have been taken.
- All the required pre-bookings are done.
- The necessary communication tools are made available.
- The detailed personal information sheet that may be required during an emergency is made ready.
- First aid, basic food & beverage, dress, and medicine kits are made ready.

Every trip is a happiness enhancer for you. This faith will help you become happier.

****

Don't miss out!

Visit the website below and you can sign up to receive emails whenever Khagesh Mahanta publishes a new book. There's no charge and no obligation.

https://books2read.com/r/B-A-KFHO-SNVNB

BOOKS2READ

Connecting independent readers to independent writers.

Table of Contents